# THE DARK SIDE

# MY PERSPECTIVE

DEPRESSION
ANXIETY
SELF BELIEF
SELF DOUBT
SELF AWARNESS
BULLYING
RESPECT

WRITTEN BY
JASON FITZGERALD

The Dark Side
My Perspective

ISBN: 978-0-9876384-5-8   paperback
ISBN: 978-0-9876384-7-2        ebook

Copyright © Jason Fitzgerald 2018

First published 2018

All rights reserved. Without limiting the rights under copyright reserved above, no part of this publication may be reproduced, stored in or introduced into a database and retrieval system or transmitted in any form or any means (electronic, mechanical, photocopying, recording or otherwise) without the prior written permission of both the owner of copyright and the above author.

# Contents

*Chapter 1*
Depression. . . . . . . . . . . . . . . . . . . . . . . . . . . 1

*Chapter 2*
Anxiety . . . . . . . . . . . . . . . . . . . . . . . . . . . . . 8

*Chapter 3*
Self Belief, Self-Doubt & Self Awareness . . . 13

*Chapter 4*
Bullying . . . . . . . . . . . . . . . . . . . . . . . . . . . 19

*Chapter 5*
Respect . . . . . . . . . . . . . . . . . . . . . . . . . . . 24

Notes: . . . . . . . . . . . . . . . . . . . . . . . . . . . . . . 28

So, this book is not a how to do it, or written by a specialist. I have no formal qualifications; hence why this book, is not written as a text book.

So, why write this book, simply I have struggled and dealt with or seen all of this. So, why not write about my view, my perspective, in the hopes, readers will gain some understanding of knowing it's not just them.

These are all misconstrued or falsely misunderstood facets of life. Usually, those who can't see them, do not believe them or are quick, to say, "well if you did this, etc."

So, during each chapter, I endeavor to give a better insight into these. I like to call these, dark diseases.

*Chapter 1*

# Depression

Depression to me is a dark disease. Now do not get me wrong, although no cure exists, systems are in a place to help manage or to cope with depression.

How often; do you come across a person you know or meet who tells you they suffer from depression? You think, well are they just saying it for sympathy?

What about those, who say nothing, and you are none the wiser. The fact is that many, have depression. You, can't see it all you can do is assume, guess or find out after the fact.

I have had depression since I was a young teen. I didn't know; that's what it was. Or, that when diagnosed it could be treated. What I thought; I had was justified anger and a bad understanding of me.

That's right; I believed I was the issue. That I caused, the thoughts in my head. Based on how I looked at events or the way people dealt with me.

Now, I had awesome friends and some great family, but it doesn't help; so, I thought. I would as often phrased; bottle things up, I believed, I had no one to talk too.

I was also under the assumption if I dared speak of what I had going on in my head. People would judge me and criticize me.

I was right, to a point, so many made assumptions; based on interactions with me. Things I said or did, added fuel to the fire inside my head. The more I heard these things, the more; I converted them; to become a belief and an attack on myself.

At the age of 17, I made attempts to end my life. My thoughts, my issues, for once and all; would be gone. The first instance, I took a full packet of Panadol, with straight cordial. That was the concoction; I had, believed would do it.

What it did, was send me, on an absolute spin out. I was sleepy, incoherent, the last thing, I remembered, was my door (yes, at 15 I had moved, out of the family home, by this time I was living in a self-contained unit) was kicked in.

My friends, at that time in my life, came through the door; with the ambulance officers. They took me to the hospital, where they took care of me.

Now, you're wondering, what was in my head; to make me do such a thing. Without writing, a whole book, leading up to it - there was a multitude of factors.

So, while I am in the hospital, being evaluated. My parents had been informed, of what I had done, to myself. I was not stable enough, mentally, to be on my own, so I got released into my parent's care.

Now, the doctors had no clue; what my issues where. I wouldn't, discuss them either. Before this attempt, I had some blood tests and other tests, to try

## Chapter 1   Depression

and diagnose, why I was having, these little blackouts and partial fits.

So, I was released, into my parent's care. Although still awaiting results, I was not, to be not left alone. My stepfather took me to work with him. So, he could try and talk with me, and keep an eye on me.

While, sitting in his truck, at one of his customers. He was doing his job. Meanwhile, he kept coming and would check on me. Bang, I pulled, my pocket knife, from my belt, opened it and cut across my wrists.

I wanted out, of this world, it was all I could think of at this time. My stepfather wrapped my wrists, with rags and drove straight to the hospital. Luckily, for me I had no clue; what I was doing, so the damage was minor but, in my head, I felt cheated.

So, the hospital admitted me again, to keep an eye on me. Now, you're thinking, at this stage surely; I am through hurting myself; well no, apparently not.

The next day, the doctor comes in, and said to me "the results are back, my tests show, from there research, they believed I had epilepsy'. Now with this diagnosis comes changes.

I was not allowed, to drive anymore. I was 17, I just, got my learners, a big thing for a teen. I was also, not allowed, to do a pile of other things. In my head, I had shut off, after hearing, I could no longer drive.

So, I was released, told to go home, not to do anything silly. I had an appointment, with a counselor, that afternoon, just up, from where I lived.

Now, this is the first time; I had been, to my unit since the first attempt. So, when I got home, I started cleaning, my unit and then chilled out watching tv.

The next thing, I remember, is getting up off, the bed. I had to see this counselor; it was then, I noticed the new medication; I had obtained, that morning for epilepsy.

The bottle was open; some pills were on the table. But when I picked up the pills and placed them back, I could clearly, see the bottle was missing heaps.

Yes, I had overdosed again; with no recollection of doing so. I do not, even remember doing anything; but laying on the bed watching tv. So, I head up to a counselor; she is not there; I am sitting on the steps, getting droopy- when she arrived. She could see, I was not right.

I explained, my pill bottle, was missing a few tablets. The counselor quickly grabbed them from me, counted them, I had taken 48 of these pills. She called, the ambulance; they told her, there was no time to wait, for them. She loaded me in the car, and drove to the hospital, as fast as she could.

When we arrived at the hospital, I was barely coherent. I was unstable, on my feet, the nurses (as well, as the ambulance staff, who had met us at the hospital) placed me on a stretcher. I remember, being pushed up the ramp, to the emergency section, I counted one, two lights and then nothing.

Right now, you're thinking holy shit. You would be right; I had succeeded, this time, at ending my life. I was out and gone, of course, I wasn't as successful, as I thought because of the doctors and nurses were good.

Now, this next little bit, has some bits, from family and friends. Nana worked at the hospital; she knew a

## Chapter 1  Depression

major emergency, was happening but had no idea it was me, right there, at that moment.

She told me later, she and other staff, as well as patients, heard this almighty, bellow echo through the hospital. Everyone wondered, what was going on.

I was fighting, with everything; to stop the nurses and doctors from restraining me. They were trying, to get lifesaving equipment connected.

Nana wandered down, to see what was happening, she was informed, it was me and serious, of course, she rang my parents.

Later that evening, I was in ICU, stable, but not out of the woods yet. Now, we lived in a country town, so medical equipment was not always the best.

During the ordeal, I had vomited, as I breathed in at the same time; this caused, an acidic fluid, to be in my lungs, which caused Pneumonia.

It was now, also making me worse. So, I was shipped, the first thing the next day, via ambulance to a small airport, just out of town. I was, flying to the next town, I had many relapses, during all this. Eventually, I was stabilized, but I was in an induced coma.

My friends, were apparently, on their way to my nanas house. On the day I was, transported to see if I was with her; as they couldn't find me. When the ambulance, drove past them, with their, lights going, they jokingly said: "I wondered if that's Jason."

Well, when they arrived at Nana's house, they nearly dropped dead, when they found out it was me; in the ambulance and what had happened.

Now, I could continue with this story, but I think you get the idea. I survived, as I am, writing this book, but the depression has never left me.

Now, I am 43 a few weeks off 44 when writing this and I still battle every day with depression, I have been at times medicated for it, and only two years before writing this I had gone downhill fast because of it again.

I had become reclusive; hardly ventured to anywhere outdoors. But I sought help this time; before I did anything - stupid to myself.

You cannot ever get people to understand; what goes on, in one's head with depression. We battle daily, with all kinds of thoughts. It takes a lot of effort, for us to get up each day; and go on, to smile, to socialize; to be a part of our community.

It's even harder, for us to ask for help; or admit defeat to others, but mostly to ourselves. Now do not get me wrong, depression can also make us great, how you ask?

Well by using the depression, as a tool for life, it can make us stronger. Circumstances, that other people cannot handle; we can find ourselves, enjoying being a part of something - because we can be the person, we are not inside, but on the outside; like an actor.

Depression can also make us feel; we are not a part of society. That is how we feel because others cannot understand us. We can't say or do things, to make you understand, or not to judge us.

Depression is a disease; no matter what anyone says, yes you can manage it at times. You can never defeat it, no matter what self-help books are out there.

## Chapter 1   Depression

Just because a specialist, says it that way; because a textbook, states it.

If you come across, someone with depression; please never judge us. Do not try to fix us. Treat us normally, be an ear; when we need it. Be that helping hand that picks us up; when we fall.

If your reading this; because you suffer, from the mental illness, called depression. Seek help; you're not alone, you are not different to anyone else.

These days, there are more services, than ever before; use them not for anyone else - but yourself.

Associate with people, who are there for you. Never be with the ones that will tell you, how it should be. The people that you have in your life can be the reason you take control of your depression and not give in to it.

Depression is a heredity disease!

*Chapter 2*

# Anxiety

Some people believe anxiety is fear; it's far from it. Many people associate it, with depression; it's not associated with depression. Anxiety is the body's alarm system that has become so touchy; it goes off all too often.

Yes, medical practitioners can give you medication. It helps to control it, but other factors play a part of it - that you, need to control.

Anxiety makes you feel nauseous, light-headed, your heart beats faster; everything feels rushed and overwhelming. What causes this, mostly it will be factors in your brain.

How you see a situation; or you have been involved, in a situation. Your brain is setting off alarms, that warn you constantly. When you over think, a situation you become; stressed and can't focus, on how to control - the feeling, this is anxiety.

It is not your fault; you are not bizarre. You have, an over-stimulated brain; that processes everything, in a different way.

## Chapter 2  Anxiety

We get described, as hot-headed; or an overreactor, simply because, we process things different to others.

Can we get pass anxiety? Yes. Until we learn, to control our brain and thoughts; of course, we cannot control everything, every single time.

People try to tell you; it's all in your head. Well hello; we are fully aware of that. Otherwise, we wouldn't have the condition.

Stimulants can increase the anxiety; making us feel overwhelmed, in situations, we have no control over.

Strangely enough, some people associate anxiety; with OCD. It is far, from true; at times, we self-diagnose, ourselves of being OCD; because of anxiety.

As I have gotten older; my anxiety changes. My stimulant is coffee; I love coffee. Another condition is called control disorder.

Now, do not misconstrue, control disorder with a control freak. These are two different issues, with some similarity.

I have control disorder, people have called me a control freak. It's not about controlling others, like your partners every movement. Control disorder is about controlling, your movements, situations, your environment.

See for me; this aggravates my anxiety, my poor wife and children; endure so much because of it.

I cannot control it, or get rid of it. I do warn others, about it and turn it into a joke.

But sometimes, to me, it's not a joke. I am, who I am; and the way I am, as I age, it's getting worse.

See even a sandwich, can set me off. Why do you ask? Because I have a way, I like it made and I don't change my method, of what I like.

Everything has a place; it belongs in that spot. Therefore, people confuse it with OCD. Now, OCD is usually a numerical disorder; where everything has a way, how many times, it could be done; not always number based, but primarily.

Someone may close and lock a door, ten times before they compute; the door secured. Whereas, me I will get anxious, because a person, did not shut a door, lock a door, or open it, and latch it back. It's not numerical, in a sense, it's about the way, things should be the first time.

It's how it works, is used; or should be. Sounds trivial, to others; but to me, it's not. How I control, my environment is important to me.

See a control freak, is someone, who can't let their partners do something. They must know, all their movements, messages, etc; this is not acceptable.

My wife can go and do what she likes anytime. Yes, I get concerned, if she is late home; If I have not heard, from her for a period. I trust her; I do not trust; the environment.

I cannot stay calm, when someone messes, with my environment; this is a part of the anxiety.

If you move something or do not put it back; to its original location, I get anxious and angry.

I do not handle change, at that very moment, it occurs. Although I can react in an emergency, that's different.

## Chapter 2  Anxiety

If I work, in an office and someone moves my desk, or you come to work, and the boss says "today, you're going to do this, or that."

It will change, what's in my head, I will get anxious, because, you have changed my environment.

I must control my environment; everything has a system, I can adapt to the change after a period, which can be, an hour or a day. But then that change becomes the new norm for me.

One time, I had a stepdaughter, from a previous relationship. Her room was always messy; getting her to clean it, was always an issue. Her excuse was because she's too lazy.

I said to her "I am the laziest person you will ever meet!", She replied "Bullshit; you are always doing something, even cleaning something." (This is not OCD this is, control disorder by the way)

I replied, "yes, and that's why I am lazy, I do not create jobs for myself, I put things away and keep my environment clean." "This is so I can spend, more time being lazy, instead of sitting there and looking at something, knowing that I have that job to do; hence why I am the laziest person here."

She thought about that for a bit, then cleaned her room. Years later after having left home and lived with her boyfriend, she was over for dinner, comes to me and says, "I hate you." I said, "why? What have I done now?" She replied, "I have become you, I am now the lazy person you are, and everyone hates it; but I can't stand a mess or things not being where they should be," we both laughed so hard.

So, anxiety is a result of other factors; it attaches itself to your ways and thoughts. You cannot cure it, but you can adapt to It, once you learn when and how it will appear.

You cannot be aware of every time or circumstance. Sometimes, you cannot cope, right at that time of reaction, but you can keep changing when you learn how to manage it.

*Chapter 3*

# Self Belief, Self-Doubt & Self Awareness

Self-belief & self-doubt, unfortunately, go hand in hand. We often believe we can do or achieve something. Although straight away, we doubt if our thoughts or intentions are correct.

You always look at something and quiz yourself; can you do it? If so how? And then say, "if I do this or that could I bugger it up."

So, at times we then choose to employ, hire or learn something, to do things, that we cannot see ourselves doing.

Of course, we cannot do everything, even though we believe we can; usually because of lifestyle, financials or laws and regulations.

People often need a trigger, from somewhere or someone, to believe we can do something. When we try to achieve something, then others can be the reason we doubt ourselves.

Take losing weight as an example; all your friends and family rally beside you saying, "you can do it! Believe in yourself, because we believe in you".

Or they say the opposite, "you cannot lose weight; because your lifestyle won't change."

You can be happy, with your life. Sometimes someone else, believes they know all, about your issues and how to fix it. They will doubt you have the tenacity to do it.

How can we believe, in ourselves without doubting ourselves? Well first, you must take control of you; do not listen to other influences.

You need to be you, reality says you cannot, be anyone else, other than you. We can all portray ourselves, as something else, till we tire of it.

You need to be strong; you need to stand up, for yourself; this is believing in yourself, doubts are our little arguments, we will have to deal with them.

Other times we can have the right people, around us. These people don't tell you, what you can and cannot be. They believe in themselves; this often rubs off on you. You can grasp this energy; it makes you want; to strive to become more.

It doesn't matter if it's your home life, work life or social life. You will have these back and forth thoughts, or judgments against others.

We are all different, we all have different strengths or measures, but how we cope and control them is up to us.

I cannot tell you how to do this; my methods may only suit me. They may also encourage you, to look at yourself in other ways.

### Chapter 3   Self Belief, Self-Doubt & Self Awareness

You know, I grew up loving trucks, motorbikes, fishing, boating the list goes on; but I had to believe if I wanted to be me, I could do them.

The same when it comes to sports, the other team cannot make me play better. They can show me their way if it works great; if not I change, what I learn to suit me.

We all have different calibers of friends, in our lives. Some make us feel better, some make us feel inadequate, some are just on the same page as ourselves.

I find as I am getting older, we often tolerate someone else. It may be, a partner of a friend, or we can see something, in them, they can't see, in themselves. By having them around, balances ourselves out.

Look at churches; people go there because they believe, in something greater. Other people avoid them because they don't believe, in there being something greater.

When writing this book, I had to believe, I could not only write something but that people would read as well as purchase it. Even as I write this sentence, I doubt if it will succeed; or that I can even publish it.

I have at times in my life, been told to write a book, about what I know or have experienced. People believed in me; I didn't believe, it was something others would want to buy to read.  I have doubted myself, for years.

Did I have what it would take to write; would I get writer's block; or would it become be a load of crap on paper?

I still don't know, because I am writing it. I have not published it, to know. I have no formal training to be a writer, but I decided, to believe, in me.

Over the last few months, I started running ideas and formats through my head. I quizzed myself if this could get it done; should I do it? Now I will see what happens if nothing else; at least for me I will know, "I written a book."

So, I sat at my desk, doing my usual check emails and other bits and pieces. Then I opened, word and looked for a book format. I googled the internet looking at how I even go about writing a book and publishing it.

Next thing, I was typing a title, then a chapter and then another and so on until I had written my first book. Every day I sat and wrote and reread and added bits and edited it.

Then I finished it; I was like ok what now. More research on how to publish, these days you have an eBook as well as hard copies, the choices are numerous.

My understanding was you had to send your final draft, to a publisher. Then wait and see if they liked it and took it on board. Now you can register yourself, thanks to the internet, with companies that help you self-publish.

But I still doubted, what I am doing. I have second guessed it, will people buy it and read it? Then while working all that out, a few days later; I just decided to write this book. Meanwhile, the other book was sitting in my files, on the computer.

I still doubted; if I can get to the next step. I believe I have something people will enjoy reading. My first book, I sent some copies; to some of my family to have a read. Trust me, I have the kind of family, that if its crap; they will tell you. Some friends or family may sugar coat it because they are your family.

Now for me, I thought ok; they are busy people, it may take a few weeks to get through it. It was not because it was 1000 pages, because it is not that big; way less actually. But because these family members are very busy people.

Now my Aunty, who I can always, get an honest opinion from; I messaged her and said, "hey, I wrote a book, nothing flash, this is just a draft, still editing and so forth; would you like to read in your spare time and provide feedback?

Now she replied, she would be interested to read it. Anyway, a few hours go by, I get an email from her, saying, "I am reading in amongst my work, and I am about halfway through; will finish when I can, you know what I think? So far it is brilliant! I'm impressed!"

Now firstly I was shocked, that she had gotten into it straight away. I was even more shocked, to have had her respond in that way.

Now if you doubt yourself, most times you will miss an opportunity, or never achieve something. You must, take steps at times, to believe in yourself and have a crack, regardless of your doubts.

Now listen, I am not an expert, on anything in this book. I am simply sharing my views, expressions, and snippets of my life; as to why these things happen or matter, especially to me.

All this falls, under self-awareness as well. Because once, you're aware of you, your strengths and weakness, you can achieve whatever you set yourself to achieve.

Do not let other people bring you down. We do that ourselves, often enough; so, start being aware of you and start believing in you, stop doubting yourself.

*Chapter 4*

# Bullying

Bullying! I hate it! I cannot tolerate it.

Our future, although being made more and more aware of bullying and its effects. It is thanks to social media, it's now everywhere and prominent in our lives.

Yes, it should be spoken about, not hidden. Yes, with the internet, things can be seen much quicker; but this same tool and other programs designed on the internet, are also contributing to the bullying epidemic.

There are, many different types of bullying, cyber, physical, emotional or mental abuse, the list can go on. But what creates bullying, that's the main issue.

We are not robots; we are not all the same, how boring would it be if we were? God made us all different, or some higher power did, whatever your belief is.

People hate change; they hate someone who is different from them or those that will not follow them. Some people want to be popular; some want to remain hidden, some want acceptance.

The backdrop of what instigates bullying has many factors; it can be a mindset, beliefs, home life, the people we surround ourselves with, jealousy this list can go on.

Now just because, one of these factors; unleashes something in you to act in this way, it does not give you any right to belittle, target, harass or attack someone else ever!

If you do not like something, someone, because it's not your belief, walk away keep it to yourself. You do not have the right to inflict insult or injury to someone else.

Often people target those, they think are worse than them, below them, weaker, or in some way different to them.

It is not right; it can never be fixed, until others speak up, stand up, educate their children and friends that bullying is not ok and that we won't tolerate it.

Why should another individual have to endure this treatment? Why should they be forced to feel different, or weird just because someone or a group says so? Why do many of these people, take their own lives; when they are not at fault.

They take their lives, in many circumstances because that is, the only escape they see. In previous chapters I spoke about depression, anxiety these are sometimes, the result of bullying.

We can't just blame bullies, at times its lack of education, understanding, peer pressure or a reaction to having been bullied, in some way themselves.

Everybody has the right to be free, to feel accepted and to be a part of this world. We have the right to be free in our own homes and these days on social media, without being attacked.

The other name for bullies, on social media, is trolls, a name given to those who often, extremely opinionated, to their beliefs, that are different to someone else's.

Our homes, our phones, our social media accounts, should be a way to be with friends or family and to be a haven. We should feel that safety, in other places of this world too, but there are still crimes we cannot control.

It can be so easy for us to sit and judge, the victim or the abuser without any fact. Try getting to know them before you sit and judge, make sure you are perfect, before making a judgment.

Just because someone is obese, handicapped looks different laughs different dresses different does not mean they are any less of a person than you. Just because you have good looks, wealth, style, does not mean you're better than anyone else.

That person, you bully may be the doctor, nurse or scientist you may need later in life. That person who bullied you maybe the homeless person you serve at a soup kitchen, one day because they lost everything, they once had.

We change at all stages, of our lives, sometimes for the better, sometimes for the worse. But you cannot ever predict what the future holds, but we can predict one thing; bullying leaves a long-term effect on life.

Take time to get to know someone, just because a person is popular, does not mean they are perfect. Often, it's their way, to cover the flaws they do not want you to see, and by bullying you, it takes the focus off them.

Some people support and laugh with the bully, that doesn't make them any different to the bully. The effect it has, and those same people are often easily misled or fake and are hiding, behind that premise to avoid being a target.

If you see someone that is being bullied, usually they have been singled out, or become a minority, compared to the number of people propping up the bully. Remember safety in numbers, so stand up with the target the more support, they get the sooner the bully looks elsewhere or loses interest.

No, it's not right, but if everyone, takes a stance against a bully, including their entourage, then bullying can and will stop.

We have slowly, introduced laws in Australia against bullying, we have a stand up to bullying day, we have education resources at hand, but the bullying is not stopping why?

Because when it is time to deal with it, our hands are tied legally, you can't touch a bully; you cannot always prove you got bullied because people won't be a witness.

Schools have anti-bully rules, yet often the victim is not heard, the parents of the bully, support their child; because they are ignorant to the facts, "their child does not bully anyone" they say.

It is so easy to ignore, or make it not as severe as it is, but what you don't see; is what is happening internally to the victim: the hurt, the pain, the betrayal, the disbelief, and the judgment on themselves.

So how do we stand up? How can we stop it; well firstly, we need to educate our children, from a young age, disrupt bullying behavior, be firm, that it is not ok.

Listen to the victim, trust the victim, build trust with the victim, especially as a parent so they can feel safe in coming to you. Not only telling you but show you, when it happens, via texts or other forms via social media. If they receive calls, make them answer it near you; so, you hear it firsthand.

Every time a child suicides, from bullying we lose someone, who may have made a difference in this world, had they been given a chance.

Start accepting others, are different to you, having someone different or opposite to you as a friend, may change your whole way of life and vice versa.

Support one another, no matter what it is, that victim, who happens to dress tacky may have a bad home life. Unfortunately, it is often the case, that they will be forgotten a lot of the time. Support them, share lunch, so they don't starve, give them clothes you no longer wear, the options are endless.

Include them stop excluding them!

*Chapter 5*

# Respect

Respect, simple word, with so much meaning. It's often used incorrectly or not at all. Education is the key to understanding respect and changing our world.

We have an obligation, to respect others, no matter what. Even if it seems you have different views. Yes, there are situations, respect goes out the window, unfortunately.

It is often said, "Give respect - get respect." Do to others, as you would want to happen to you, or give no respect, when receiving no respect.

Of course, you cannot please everyone, or every situation, just by having or using respect. If someone disrespects you, how can you show respect?

Some say you must be the bigger person sometimes, and that person shall judge themselves later. Now this will not happen every time in life, but education is the key, and it starts with you.

So often these days we see much disrespect, people are disrespecting their partners, through domestic violence, disrespecting authority at school or in the community. Abusing powers, by expecting; to be respected but not show the same courtesy to you.

Due to our economics, we see a growing attack on others, home invasions, thefts, random assaults, this is not respect. Desecrating graves, disrespecting veterans, disrespecting our elderly.

When did we forget, that the reason we are here or can enjoy the things, is because of those who came before us?

Respect can often be used as a weapon, by disrespecting others. It can be used to grow with others, by showing respect.

Some people have it their heads that they deserve respect, it's all about them. Often, they will not give a person, who should be respected, the respect they deserve.

Kids in school these days are prime examples. I am not saying all kids, but back in my day; if you disrespected a teacher, you got the cane. These days you are sent to the office, school rings parents, parents take the child home, school tells parents that child is disrespectful and a nuisance, solves nothing.

It will not educate your children, by sending them away from school, it will teach them how to beat the system. I do understand; after all, the do-gooders are jumping up and down; laws have been changed to accommodate the disrespect, as they are not held liable for their actions.

Of course, I do not condone excessive punishment, but I do believe, a bit of firmness, to get the respect you deserve, is not too much to ask.

What goes through a person's mind when attacking or robbing the elderly? Is it because they seem to be weaker and easier to target?

When does a person look at a frail elderly person and say, "that's who I am going to disrespect today"? Yes, some of the oldies can be very forthwith about views, but respect the fact, that they grew up in a harder culture, where things were different.

As the saying goes, "it is hard to teach an old dog new tricks." Well, it seems, to be getting harder to teach young pups as well.

Respect is the key; it plays its part in society, how we learn, by not having respect, or using it, turns our society upside down.

Respect plays its roll in every chapter, of this book, it forms the good and bad of every situation. If we cannot respect ourselves and others, then how will our future turn out.

Now I am not an angel, when I was a child, I disrespected it's the way of learning, our way through society and finding our place. If I was caught disrespecting teachers at school, I got the cane at home; I got disciplined.

I grew up knowing, that respect is key to life, the more you use it, in its purpose the more things happen. Using manners is something slowly dying, from our teachings. Well, I have taught my children and stepchildren that manners are a major form of respect to others.

Now I cannot control, my children's ways completely, but they know the right from wrong and who, and when respect and manners are to be used.

## Chapter 5  Respect

I know one thing, I cannot stand, is the disrespect for other people's properties. Our elderly suffer from, the crimes of disrespect every day.

To the disrespecting people, in our community; just because your life is hard, or so you believe it is harder than someone else's. It does not give anyone the right to touch anyone's possessions.

Lastly, we need to start to start standing up and respecting ourselves.

**Notes:**

**Notes:**

**Notes:**

**Notes:**

**Notes:**

www.ingramcontent.com/pod-product-compliance
Lightning Source LLC
Chambersburg PA
CBHW050608300426
44112CB00013B/2133